# Karst Mountains
# Will Bloom

# Karst Mountains Will Bloom

*The Collected Poems*

*of*

*Pos Moua*

**Blue Oak Press**
Rocklin | California

Cover design by Maxima Kahn
Cover painting: *Zos Roob Tsua Zeb*
By Boon Ma Yang
Interior design by Sarah Miner
Typeset in Centaur

Printed and bound by Bookmobile
Printed in the United States

Library of Congress Cataloging-in-Publication Data
has been applied for
Moua, Pos
*Karst Mountains Will Bloom* by Pos Moua

ISBN 978-0-9975040-2-6

## Dedications

These poems are dedicated to my wife, Mao Lee, and to my children: Lewg, Serena, Luna, Sher Yin, Forest; to all my sisters: Yia, Mai Yang, Candy, Lisa, Yer, Amanda, Kaxia, Rachel; to Brother Long and Baby Leng; to Tong Ying Vang and Dr. Tru Chang and all my other brothers, sisters, and friends; and to all who are traveling through this cosmic journey with me. May your beautiful intent to love all and endure the many miles ahead be a blessing in all your mornings and evenings.

# CONTENTS

## III   Ashes, Dreams, and Rebirth

## IV   Mountain Spirits

# Foreword

The English language has a short history. Hmong is a language (and a people) of great antiquity that was well established in southern China even before "Chinese." Qing dynasty pressure started driving the Hmong south into Thailand, Viet-nam, and Laos about five hundred years ago. Many live in South China still, getting a bit more respect today, and still called Hmong or Miao.

During the Southeast Asian wars many Hmong left Asia by slipping across borders, including Pos Moua ("Baw Mwa") as a lad. A portion of his large family clan got through and they, with many other Hmong refugees, settled in Merced, California.

Pos' intellectual gifts and artistic potential were recognized by the University at Davis and that's where he and I first met years ago— "Creative Writing, Poetry." His freedom with Americano and his broad vocabulary, the acquaintance with poetics and devices in American writing amazed me. At the end of the term his chapbook—"Where the Torches Are Burning"—was complete.

Almost twenty years later Randy White of Blue Oak Press sent me the MS of *Karst Mountains Will Bloom*. Sandra McPherson and Alan Williamson had worked with Pos and found his work a surprise and a delight.

I'll insert my own particular delight here. It has to do with love. The occidental culture has said plenty over the centuries about romance, love, and family. It wasn't until I ventured in certain non-western so-cieties and realized they had fresh and surprising ways of living and loving that I saw that there were more poetic worlds to explore. The Hmong and related societies are well-known in Asia to have a vivid love-life and large and active families. Even Marco Polo wrote a bit on this. Pos who is now in his late forties, and his wife Mao (about the same age) have five children. The family is still strong and together. There are entire Hmong communities in America now with this spirit and persistence but also exploring and learning the new society they've dropped into. There are poems that show us unconventional, deeply true ways of expressing attraction, affection, to others. "I have practiced long and hard not to remember you."

Much more will be found in these poems. Karst is a geologists' term for a type of land-surface and subsurface of heavy, water-soluble rock, porous and producing pools and caves, with soils that can be inspiring, confusing, and productive.

Making the tough landscape bloom is a real poetic accomplishment; so is nourishing a language and its people in a new place and to do it all in one generation. Pos Moua brings another original voice to Turtle Island.

GARY SNYDER

# About Karst Mountains

We are those who were forced out of our homes after many centuries of warfare. We are the Hmong, a subgroup of the indigenous Miao people of south China. Our ancestral lands are drained by the great rivers: the Yangtze, Mekong, Irrawaddy, Pearl, and Red, our villages and fields beside the limestone pinnacles of the karst mountains and hills. This always remains foremost in the mind of every Hmong.

I was born among these karst mountains and lived part of my childhood high up on those inconsolable ranges. Now, far away, I feel those mountains lingering in my heart. I still yearn to return to them. I once heard a wise, elder woman say, "It is prophesied that when we mortals have seen karst mountains bloom, it is then that the hour of love and peace will have permeated the sky and earth with a flood wave like none before." This was etched into my psyche since youth. My sister died in those mountains. My grandmother and grandfather, my aunts and uncles, and my cousins, and almost all my father's family died during the Secret War, their deaths too sad for me to write about.

The title for this collection came to me because my friend, the poet Soul Vang, translated one of my Hmong poems into English. He rendered the Hmong phrase *"tsua zeb yuav tawg paj"* into "karst mountains will bloom." This translation rightfully became the title for a reading the Hmong American Writers' Circle organized, calling on Hmong poets and writers across America to participate in it. It was a celebration for emerging Hmong writers, opening a path for the rebirth of our cultural practices and storytelling. It was a means of reincarnation for us. So, let us return to the mountains and rivers and the freedom to live well with one another, to care for this Earth, and to balance the space between joy and grief, discontinuity and flow, birth and no-birth.

In my poem, "Karst Mountains Will Bloom," the key verse in Hmong is *"Tab sis yog koj hlub kuv, tsua zeb yuav tawg paj"*: ("But if you love me, karst mountains will bloom"). This is the Hmong's prophetic, declarative announcement of love (and sometimes loss), of the truth that binds mortals to nature's unceasing, unyielding course. To me, it is the impossible made possible. Literally, karst rock cannot bloom in the human time perspective, but viewed from the geological time perspective, it can bloom—like mountains walking. Our mountains represent home, time, and space for me—yes, mountains stand for struggles and war, like the ascent, the tragic climb. But they are also beautiful and inconsolable to me. Mountains live in deep time in the way that I do not, yet in the way that I wish I could have lived my life. I would like to think that.

POS MOUA

# I

## The Old Country

# Poem from Laos

*for Mai Zoua*

Your heart isn't an eloping
spirit and should not now
hide under rocks, under
unforgiving crevices, so far
away, way back into

days when we were native
grass, dried among the rice
in the makeshift granaries: and we who
were imaginary were munching on
warm, supple hand-patted
rice bread and the

thought gave fatigue the will to
crawl back inside our stomachs
and we cried out like two silent, caged
proboscis monkeys, desperate to be bees

and my hands tremble too like
two wrens caught in the cosmic
fire ring—one side, no
country; the other, the
mountains towering, bombs

shattering hills and trees, while the river
torrentially spilled over the cliff
down under our feet—famishing
you further more than me; each
nap unknowingly was
a long night, till the afternoon robins
awakened us, for fatigue,

another form of hunger, always
found its way back to our
unrequited sleep—for the many

miles I could have borne
you, I could have been your
carriage, but in my mind my
body besieged me to

set you down; would
the hills carry us with
you on my skinny
back? But you, my love

were kind to me,
saying, the withering
flowerings in your tone,
"Set me down,
my brother; let me
walk," yet I knew it in your eyes,
how little your feet were,

emaciated among the boulders
of the forest floor, and I replied,
"I must, you get on my back,
it is you I must carry, the bombs
are unkind, raining down, sounds

of guns approaching fast, if
not we'll be the forest," so then I
held you close to me,
on my back, and the sun
once again lingered, hovered above,
like hunger: it was

not hard to see the wet
corners of your eyes when the grayish
trails through those woods are
dust forged from your bones.

## Our Hour of Expatriation

*with Paoze & Zang*

What are memories left to be
fermented between our young
days? These mountains and this
lake now subtly recede like
cool winds rushing over
obsidian-granite cliffs, streams
shooting into our hearts-eyes, stars
streaming down on us that we
like traveling merchants covet,
and the sun above ceases to warm.

Can we shove them down
the way we do old handmade
embroideries left behind
by Hmong grannies, who
walked with aging gait, swaying
to their own slow swinging,
like grassy Chowchilla hays?

Can we steal them, crease them
in the subdivisions of
our people like curvy strands
of long black hair left
behind on sweat-soaked pillows
after thrusts and hums, remnants
of our sweet lost lovers?

Can we transport them through
the residual spaces along highways?

How can we poise ourselves
to singe them, torch them,
electrocute them, put them in the
prisons of this country for eternity,
set them as ash on paper
boats shimmering and set adrift
into thin solemnity, as we sought
freedom through rebirth's blockades?

Must we cut them into fine
pieces and boil them on makeshift
stoves to accentuate and to enunciate
with our souls' precision those
that we could not have, those
we may not outlast?

What else can we do, if not
to seek them besides the homeless scenes?

These are tints of our being here—
the lights in the mornings
and evenings seen
on the scales of
this rainbow trout.

## Laos, 1977

Long years trotted down the passing river and field.
Some nights, tears stood in his eyes
when he was about to sleep:

He remembers sleeping warm
under the color of absence—
absence in disgrace, disgrace
from forgetting to march for the dead,
forgetting is another disgrace of absence.

Absence from killings, like the killing of the bird,
like the air killing the bird, the bird's the people—

Send these killings to the bombarded fissures,
the new design of the grass cottages,
and these are
pictures returning to you:

> a farmer's palm
> parted from his body lies on the ground which
> once held his whole body standing perfectly erect,

> fingers and hair lost
> & hanging on scorched branches.

# Open Hands and the Man with One Leg Shorter

They liked to think they were not leaving their homes
after so many centuries of inhabiting those places.
They thought of themselves as going on an unsafe passage
and they thought they would come again
as other forms of living beings—when they no longer
lived in their present bodies—to the openness of the day,
to where the sun is high and the wind whistles in the field.

But it was hard for them
to be kind and gentle to those with open hands
waiting to be filled with rice; Open Hands, the sick
crying out for those who could no longer give;
Open Hands, signs of reaching out for a way
of arriving at the river that will connect to their wandering
spirits and restore the starving hearts.
Along the road they must go.

There were only a few who were sparing enough to have
a small bag or a scorched bamboo container of corn or rice.
Carrying one of the bags meant you were unlikely to be left behind.

The man with his wife and four children were the last group
in a long trail of people going away from their old places,
and he was carrying a roasted bamboo with rice ready to eat inside it.

A crippled man skipped to him and asked, "Elder brother,
will you give a palm of rice to last me another day? I am
not in good health to keep up with the rest of the group."
Everyone could see his eyes the moment he said that.

The man, thinking of his wife and children, knew
and replied, "I will not give, for I have four children to feed.
This isn't enough to last us through these woods."

After climbing a height and crossing a brook, they stopped
to look behind, to remember who was left behind:
That man with one leg shorter than the other, he might have
been the first to lead the rest. That man, with eyebrows lowered
after being turned down, looked away, and remained there forever.

## The Passing at the Canyon

They were themselves passing, passing the man
with one leg shorter as if he was just another
stone along their path. The man was simply himself
and the stone itself was ever more sad for the man.

Having seen so many passings and their children wearied them,
the feel of the daylight soothed them when the wind,
coming from an open canyon, blew their tired faces.

To cross the canyon, without cutting around it
or without letting the soldiers discover them, they walked
on the fallen tree that bridges the two worlds.

Parents forbade their children
to look below or ever mention what was below.

Some children managed to glance
and saw what was a body, face down, wearing brightly
colored clothes, like the traditional clothes their mothers wore.

But they did not know the meaning of these colors.
They were frightened of it, lying on sharp rocks below.
The sight of this passing left the children wondering
how many more passings were left to see.

# The Old Man by the Road They Go

That old man will not die of old age, but his death
under the wet tent, roofed by banana leaves,
chilled anyone passing by.
Was it the only resting place under Heaven or
under deep hills for him, in such a time and place?

They would pass by him pretending they didn't see him,
pretending there were no ants
walking in and out of his mouth,
taking and breathing his lonely breaths away.

On this mountain road,
they passed by him
afraid he would—half dead,
half alive—chase after them.

There were those who traveled without a bag of rice.
There were those who traveled with a begging bag
and there were those who traveled without looking
back at the old man, lying there
by the side of the road,
looking at not looking.

There were those who walked forward and backward
looking only for the moon
so they could rest, thinking of who to leave behind;
and there were those who wore food in their bellies
having not a bit of compassion for the old man
who was trying to cry or speak with his innocent
but shadowed, half-awakened eyes.

This man, with his bones showing and
soft wrinkles covering his skin,
was still trying to shine his spirit
to all those who passed by;
to all those who look to cross the river without death;
to those who feared ghosts and *Pi-nyu-waih*;
and to all those who would not sing when they are left behind
with strangers—rocks, caves, or tree trunks.

He will not die of old age, abandoned
underneath those green banana leaves.

# The People beneath a Moon before the River

After long months of wandering without knowing
how the river will unfold for them,
they're people beneath a moon before the river
preparing to settle for the night
and to pray to their ancestors for a safe crossing,
like a crossing over a bridge into the clouds.
They ask in their prayers that the river will be one
which the water will open up to the land and let them
pass without fear of the unknown dead.

Their journey is like a journey towards the sun;
often the way towards it is not the way back to the home
they long for or remember nor will it be a way to return
to the days in which they could sleep quietly before
smelling the sacred and delicious first-harvested rice.
They know the way they have come will be a way of memories
etching deep into their minds and hearts.

Before they rest to watch the silence of the river
reflected above in the night sky, they would tell tales
to quiet their children. They would tell, as if there
were no war, the tale of a goddess who journeys
to the moon searching for a pond in which her
lover was held captive. But the children grow
weary, maybe they're themselves captives, of the long travel
and soon fall asleep, before the story ends.

But of all these tales they have not forgotten to include
those who would shoot them for the silver bars
they wear around their waists. Some of them might not be able to hear of
the tale about themselves meeting the river: for they do not
know if their ancestral spirits will take them.

# The Ritual before Crossing the River

Out from another dense mosquito forest,
the river lay open before the people
who traveled only by moonlight.

There, hearing the soft wave whispering
the sorrow of leaving behind their peasant life and
having lost so many—
they could see the distant torch light
burning dimly on the other side.

Above, the moon was not the same moon
which had guided them in their existence,
and reminded them of seasons to plant crops
or to bury their dead. It was a simple relief of
hunger and thirst. It was simply a full moon
to be seen in the cold, calm night
and the water was the water.

The running water is a vast river,
the dance between the spirit and the flesh,
a story about the many and the few.
Many had sailed on its fluttering surface;
some had survived, while others disappeared.
They died on this river in order to return
to the spirit realm of the Nine Dragon,
or to return to the place where
their spirits will take another life as flowers, horses,
birds, or human beings.

The people drank their first water from it.
In their legend, this river has two sources.
Those who want to know the meaning of life
must go to the one springing water, the beginning

of the Mekong—high in the mountains
of China—where there will be only disease.

And those who want
life in bliss, or without suffering, must drink
to return to the second source.
It is there they'll find the sorrow
of wanting forever and must never again
return to the living.

But to respect both sources, whether
they drink to return to the next life or not,
they cup water in the palms of their hands
and pour it on their heads and their children's,
touching the river with care because
they have not been touched by the water for months.
Then they rode on canoes secretly arranged
for them, gliding as if to hold close to the river,
straight toward the world where the torches are burning.

## Something about Yaw

This is what I will say to you, *Yaw*:
if I, when I, find you living
in some cottage made of long grass,
built on a freshly burned rice field,

softly will I sing into your ear canal:
*Yaw*—
    I do not count the moment
    when you & love-me grandma
    drop tears on my four-or-five-year-old head
    nor will I count the day you & father point the silver blade
    at each other's throat: father wants to go this way
    but you want to go that way—
because we were departing or something like that
and the trees in our town
    & small valley were exploding
    falling onto houses—some friends & neighbors killed—
everyone started to mourn
        and sundown became two decades.
Who knows why we must flee;
we only know we can't fly.

these moments are hard like
mountains
for me to count; so I'll simply remember them—
        for you.
There were, indeed, times when bullets can't kill us:
        you & I
   the dried up river & stream
     walking       fishing
collecting nourishing seaweed    catching one stranded
              catfish that
was trying to run away    either from us

or from the heating,
yellow sunflower in the sky.

I remember your shoes,
made in the city, as precious for your feet
as white and gold fish are for the hungry body—

precious      for nobody in our valley
                    ever had shoes like yours:
my feet      bare
still show scars made by bamboo
from the time when we went to cut them to make baskets.
      one more long evening (a time when a bullet can't kill us)
      silent under the clear, summer moon,
      you showed me a ceremony of music
      in torch-light surrounding a pond—
putting a round squash bowl upside down on the water surface,
you, my rhythm *Yaw*, made sounds out of the pond

like when you were chanting
during your journey
or into the land of the shamans—
      rhythms sounding like distant *Kodo* drums
      water vibrating      frogs jumping
      soothing      the whole lonesome pond

there were many times
when a bullet can't kill us:

      I remember you telling me
      your tree under the moon shadow poetry.
simply  because I believe you might still be out there,
farming rice, boiling rice on the hand-made fire
as usual—
or because I believe you might be, slow as a tortoise,

digging tiny holes to catch delicious, golden
crickets (when you roasted them)
right now—

& so I will say to you as I've said before:
these were times when you were young as life,
standing close to me.

# Before, When We Were Not Yet Here

Before, when were not yet here,
we were in the air riding
the eagle with metal wings
and spinning beak

I detested my father then
yet I love him
for making fools of our faces—
                communicating our thirst
and hunger to the Amelica
by wriggling his fingers
into his mouth

                making signs of water,
                coca-cola, and
                orange juice;
                rice and beef

without his hands,
his entire language was like
a one-year-old babbling sounds
to the Amelica

                *Nae pua mua dae ha-our thia*
                *Nqai mo no o-?*
                *tho pue dae pae ha-our* *
                my father begged
                with his head nodding
                like a bird eating seeds

he was asking for too
little, fearing the Amelica
will not have enough for all of us

the Amelica could not reach my father's
mind, so he asked my father, "you,
something, in throat?" He said it as if
an apple got caught in his own throat
"i,don't,know,
you,want,something?"

I thought my father was an idiot
creating unknown signs
and singing echoes to the Amelica.

But that was before,
when we were not yet here.

## Leoi, Thailand, 1979: Re-Entrance to the City

Playing a game
of sandal
toss and rubber band

shots, he threw
his left sandal
through an opening

under the sky
fence and,
fearful that his

father would
beat him,
he followed his shoes,

wings folded
as if
entering an envelope,

squeezing through
the same
hole his

shoes had gone,
into a
sky of bustling

honks and
beeps,
like a moth, his wing

scales like
blue chalk
dust on the crisscross

wires, eyes
wondering at
the unfamiliar world, then

desperate for
home, his
face turned blue, heart

hauling and
pushing
boulders back up the

mountain, he
wailed at
the unexploded bombs

flowering
napalms near
their villages, turned

toward this     sun and it
blinded him, shouting like

the noise of     engines, on
his knees, trying to crawl back,

but the hole     was shaped
like the opening of a

finger trap,     but then
a gentle tapping on his

shoulder and      words were
whispered to him—

barefoot, he was      led around
concrete corners, past

loud signs, back      to the house
                      of no one's house

# Hmong Women: Their Hearts

Hmong women are expected
to carry with them many hearts:
hearts to burn in the hot sun
like a field set aflame before the planting—

hearts to cry to
in desolation and despair—
that long tear which never
seems to run dry even
in the harsh season—

hearts to cut down
bullets like the catching
of the falling petals from
a lamenting rose—

hearts to fly
beyond dark days
beyond uneven roads
beyond distance—

## China Rebirth

Look for me      among the hills
         of Yangshuo,
      the country's hearth of
   stones towering among

snow and     along buttressed walls,
grained     down by hard living, so
      many roads back to me.

Even in      the new wind-scoured
Kumtag Desert,   I am always
        China, all too
      scaly dragon
karst,

     a sway of blossom
along the Yangtze,
a heron waiting in sleet.

## Somewhere in the Cosmos

*by Burlee Vang*

Nothing but a black hole      saying
all that we cannot

& though the first law promises
that energy    never
expires

what we lose we'll keep seeing it

gone. Can you hear the universe
calling

its voice bright

& cylindrical?   Your name

is atomizing
out of moondust
gibbous

& ringed like God's throat. Some day

                          we will belong

to no constellation.   Call it our inheritance

call it something else—

this door with no corners
this room
in which we     pray  pray  pray

our heads bowed like broken satellite dishes.

Nothing to do
but let the stars          exit

the lacrimal gland.          Nothing
left here,

but all space & time

holding

every particle of you.

## Presentation

*by Sandra McPherson*

*Hello. I'm Pos.*
Night's nothing if not a window.
A child is a room, if squared.
(Children are everything if squared.)
A wife's a gate.
(Swings like a fine-carved gate.)
Pos is Pos, as he says.

*I'm Pos.* We meet.
He opens the day's door.
A mountain is there.
*Hello, I'm Pos.*

California poppies flare as do names,
or one name does for all.
*I'm Pos.* Day One.
I knew all the wildflowers
from childhood.
In no time, so did he.

Then he found the rugged city:
it needs something,
he has to give it something.
In the city he gives away his coat.
You understand? He doesn't keep it
when he has days, nights, doors,
running streams with names.

The coat just fits a cold stranger
shivering *Thank you.*

He opens night's window.
Night's closed poppies hold a name apiece.
He slips his favorite creek
under a new poem.
Water delivers it to
love's address.

And the topography of the world swerves
Pos's way.

# II

## Home and the Sierras

# By the Lake in Which I Love You

*for Mao, always*

*For me most spiritual is when I walk out to the edge of town,*
*. . . white grass rebounding in the sun,*
       *and listen to the snakes.*
   ~ Sandra McPherson

Summer was in the grass,
and summer was in this body,
this temple breathing your breath.
Summer was summer in the realness
that these branching fingers
must deliver to you, words,
memories of the lake in which I love you.

Memories of the myriad ways in which all things in a dewdrop
are delusion and realization,

the ways in which the crisp leaves,
blown by the wind of this season,
tumbled under the shade of trees,
by the lake in which I love you,

the countless visions of the sky playing
with the fallen trees,
the burnt logs, which are barren,
stirred no dying echoes,
more desolated without you,
had this lake been without you.

The tree, under whose canopy we take cover
for resurrection from the city's unfamiliar sadness,
stood only to experience the selfsame joy of treeness.
(This is the treeness of our many lives.)

Moss dried on the rocks somewhere around us,
rebounding under the open sky,
painted colors frozen under a painful sun,
only to remain beautifully brittle until the rain returns,
will disperse and glow its brilliance to other rocks.

The edible orange fern, which does not grow here,
the imaginary fern on this hill, the peak, the symbol, of no one's love,

remains and grows only in my useful memory, a reservoir of
many untraveled roads and unseen dreams.

Your hands gently winding through
my dark weeded hair felt like
the waves of sunshine in the water below.

O how is it that this place can create such a deep longing
in the remainder of my soul? And why is it that in the country
in which I long to love you even to drink all of this lake
or all of its suns will not satiate my thirst and hunger
as much as traveling through
your various soft hills, your surfaces,
when my hands are touching, holding your watery breasts?
On this summer plain, with the sun engulfing this clear pond,
the lake in which I love you,
it is not at all painful to feel the grandeur of looking
through these eyes to the sorrows outside of me—
to be quilted inside the warmth of you, of your skin,
to feel the waves in which your body moves towards mine.

It is not difficult to feel ourselves in the realm of what we see—
watching the sunlight opening the field,
reflecting colors of the lake's October shore,
grass golden as the days fading into evenings,
and I lay myself like wind-blown grass next to you
by the lake in which I love you.

# Spokane, Washington, 1980

The first time in a strange weather:
on an Indian Reservation, looking from inside
an apartment window, the cold, melting clouds
fell onto the grass outside—borderless white.

Going outside, there in the plain whiteness,
puffs from the sky landing on his face,
he loved the way he was lost in white.
But this place was haunting to him because
the people who live there sold coats and gloves,
unlike the place he was used to where neighbors
shared what they possessed when they could.

Bordered inside their own hearts,
friends left other friends waiting,
or they themselves wait to be left alone cold.
They were not happy the way they were lost.
He sometimes wanted to start a fire
that would burn out the selling of hearts and bodies,
but he knew that to burn these things is to be alien
to winter and people.

## Eating

Eating is hard.

After the cloud, months
of radiation under
    the encircling machine,

I only see the light
streaming over you—

      your torso
        an arc of the sun

the rain
inside me,

    hardening, like
      glass blue morsels.

# Off Highway 99

I roam the open country for you,
     your perfume
all along Highway 99
from Sacramento down to Bakersfield,
     and back to Merced.

Without you, a leaf cannot
     sway in the wind—blue-green
grass flow over
the range of the valley, fences
     stretch towards
     Yosemite, from Mariposa, where
     the poppies smear like faded
     colors on a poor artist's canvas.

Where you once were—under cool
     summer shade—
an old horse now waits for sun to pass.
Under the cool summer shade, your arms
     around me, the world was
     blessed, soft like your soft hair
     before the open sea—

In the open field, I stand for a long time,
     without you.

Where you were once I want
     to be stilled by
the cadence of your voice, of
what perfume rises
     from the heaving of
     your moonlit torso.

## Hornitos in the Morning

I have heard stories here of men who loved
to be with women.

Hornitos is like the way an old woman carries
her child on her back, sagging down,

sorrow in the rusted door knobs and overgrown
grass, golden by sunlight in the morning, and
in between river fogs.

Among this, among all the mornings you
have found in Hornitos, would your heart,
suspended on mourning dove wings
dance child-like alongside the river,

through the fall pain of aspens—the gold leaves
in your soul now flowing above its graves.

# An Early Morning Hike in Tuolumne

*for Tong Ying*

The path bloomed with
snow before us.

I spoke to my friend,
"Do you see

how the leaves—
frozen overnight—

are falling faster
now, where

the sunlight
touches the frost

whose hard white
had made them long

to awaken softly?"

## View from Eagle Peak

We came to    rocks piled up moony ground
gentle lichen encrusted them
     like two sponged hands
gathered in long prayer
at this stance of sky and earth.

If there had been a song,
if there had been a past,

far below     only hints of
antiquated granges with chimney
smoke rising upward,
surrounded by sparkling granites,

and even with eagle's eyes, one may
zoom     into those blazing
patches of harlequin lupine,
sketchy oak,     and dried-up ravines,

or one may sniff those
effusive pines     across valleys
and whisp beyond the living,

     feel the bed
of dreams evened.

## On Birthing

Backaches, then those nights
in the brightly lit hospital room,
the silent mantra, followed by
long months of chicken and herbs.

Our tradition desires sons,
hands that haul lumber, full sacks
on shoulders from the rice fields
and strong arms for pallbearing.

But I take my wife's hand,
look at my two daughters,
the women they are to become,
gifts of letters and songs
like their mother, and understand:
it's a slicing of body
to be a woman who loves
deeply.

# Winter

Winter wears a blue blouse
to hide a wound.

Above, a bluebird
spreads its wings;

its nest is far away
in the meadow;

now, the injured bird
is in her hands.

Her chin is on my shoulder;
her tears, a scarlet ink

on my white shirt.

# On Cedar Ridge, California

Sweetness in this mountain,
    tan warbler perched on
a branch of oak, gray
squirrels barking,
effusing pine oil in the wind,

a deer trail underneath these trees
    the way your hand slid across my cheek,
    exposing the coating greens, dancing yellows,
    fisting oranges,
       and surrendering reds—

       The cool nights setting in, after scything
& gathering the smooth grass bed
       in the field, you made for me,

    like dark pen lines over these mountain ridges.
   I drove on down to you till hunger draws me
      back to this mountain.

# Thoughts for My Wife

Most mornings, I complain
to you that I am tired,

our youngest son always crying
in the morning,

tired of the world's disasters,
cruel people and rowdy students,

the hard job of working nights
teaching, not getting things I want.

The dream of owning an egg-roll shop
is still a dream. I may never have to wake up

again, but with you, I wake to a morning
the sunlight streaming through our

bedroom windows, the world spring
again, ready for a barefoot walk along

the beach, or tip-toe in a stream
in the high mountains.

# These Would Have Been Days to Be

*for Annabel*

I believe summer will not link to summer
but will move forward and return into
these hay-stacked barns, toasting them
the color of our skin.

We would have soon disappeared, will soon disappear, closing our eyes
as though we are about to awake on another Sunday morning.
Ah, the sun would have been in your eyes & it would have been reflected out
of your hair, shining as black moth's wings.
I would have loved that—

But how could we have attached and detached,
ascended and descended each other's body for long?

We must be ever moving, making turns,
and shedding ourselves like the leaves.

The grass would again grow
and the hills, composed of sentient bones,
will soon be homes for marble-rocks,
and they too will make up a boulder
to be carved as your kid brother's gravestone.
I would have you, nothing more, then.

For you whom I've loved,
I will count our days as the burying neither of life nor of time—

These would have been days beautiful to be.

## Afterland

*by Soul Vang*

"Follow me not to that stony, macabre ancestral land
but head to the rippling, dancing sea, to mountains

capped with crispy daylight," you, my friend, said.
And I think you are right. Afterland, for me, will be

a bright seashore enfolding like a lover,
a river cascading down a mossy cliff,

spilling into a series of seven sacred pools,
finally reaching the waiting sea. But I also believe

that Afterland for you will not be stony or macabre,
but will be green, verdant mountains with rivers

and lakes full of fish, like the trout
you caught with your waning strength

in the highest lakes of the Sierra Nevada
and gifted them to me. My wife made fish soup

with carrots and Thai eggplants, spiced
with lemon grass, cilantro, and ginger.

I sipped every drop of broth, licked
clean every bone. It was heavenly!

# All Is Present

*by Yu-Han Chao*

Let us celebrate
    the gardener and his blooms
        the blushing, the spiked, those spawning
young, let us celebrate
    the first tree, axis mundi
no borders, ever-turning
leaves, boughs craning towards,
away from, vining around the center—
        weight of the world in two cupped palms.
Let us celebrate the gardener
immortal garden incarnate
boulder, soil, soul, light,
jeweled buds, mystic roots
    bless the earth, drink rain
        bind carbon into sweetness.
Mythical companions,
Kunlun Mountain
domes of jasper and jade
deaths and births, secrets and
freedom, Peach Blossom Village,
fruits of fire.
At the Jade Pool,
fish dance and nip,
flirt with silver bells.
Sunlit waves crash in hidden caverns.
    A single boat paused against
an embroidered, ten-colored horizon.
Tao Yuanming deemed it impossible
to find the way back,
rediscover those fragrant woods.
Yet, remembering, we celebrate
    the gardener, father,

teacher, fisherman
his plow, pen, love, line
bring light to
    West Paradise
dark shadows stretched long
    summer to perpetual summer.
For there is no past,
no future—time is, in spite of history,
    not linear—all is present,
present, present,
eternity right here, this moment.
Eight, ten,
two-hundred-and-sixty-thousand
immortals—fear not
for in one smile, all
shall bloom.

# III

## Ashes, Dreams, and Rebirth

# The Snow Leopard Son

My wife is standing before a snowy leopard cub,
divine child, his paws skying upward

welcoming my hands like a fancy toy, its soft coat
pulls me in, I struggle for release from its sucking pull,

I call to my wife.

We cut meat to feed it, to educate it about humans,
each piece a manner, a command.

My wife sits at the table with one of our human children;
with each feeding, he gentles but has a wildness,

grows tall and handsome, his face soft as morning, a prince
become a human, our leopard son, whom we have come to adore.

Others would kill our son for his beauty like a country full
of mountains and forests and pristine lakes.

My wife cries out, "My son!"

I wonder how we can kill what we truly love.
Our son who guards us against ghosts kindles the way we were risen

to become human.

## At the End of 5 Mile Creek Road

The long summer's heat collects
towards that creek, as it flows onward
like the chattering of old friends who
just met after long ago.

Under pine and wild berries
the ground is littered with old shotgun shells
and dark, broken beer bottles.
Where the creek continues, a cairn
of stacked rocks—green weeds grow
from inside and on top rainbow
graffiti on a palm-sized rock:
       "Good-bye Suzie Q."

As leaves fall and the creek steepens,
as a hawk on that mountain, they were.
This house of earth becomes an arc
of dust bridging towards heaven.

# The World Has Always Been beyond Me

The world has always been beyond me when
I hear the tree fall over the creek, crushing
the dark greens. I stop there before crossing
only to smell the soon forgotten smell
of camouflaged frogs, to taste the sleeping
of microorganisms I've not tasted for a long time,
living flesh other than my own,
to hold the water in the palm of my hand,
to wash away the sweat on my forehead,
like holding the wind on my face, and mostly
to touch the tree in the water that is neither
round and smooth nor rugged and coarse,
only its existence is space when all else I can't see
is sometimes spaceless in a world I cannot touch—
knowing that the world has always been beyond me
when I can walk and will no longer be able to.

But for now seeing that tree lying there like an old
deer after being shot, breathing softly to its end,
I talk to it as if I am a part of its whole.
I murmur that it shouldn't be afraid because its
once living flesh will not be used in vain as paper
in the trash, that its death will be an embodiment
of this voice, and that its remains will be shelter
for the fish and fresh water crabs. But the tree is sad,
knowing that it has been cut unlike
the human flesh where it can be bandaged or healed.
So I leave it there to sleep, to move onward,
to be recycled forever what it will be.

## Undulating Sin

I.
That night in the old car
my new, white shirt stained,
where without ritual,
we married each other.

II.
We came from the bright lucky-
unlucky machines of the casino
where lives are stashed under stones.

III.
Coming home late in the evening,
I ask you to wait for me and
not to be afraid while I fish.

You were alone,

with the guttural clucks
of the evening turkeys.

# The One Sitting on His Wooden Horse

There he is sitting on his wooden horse,
facing the altar of pain and spirits.
He has the presence of both spirit and man:
We only see him talking to us in his physical form,
but when he begins his trance to console
frightened or wandering souls, we hear him
in an archaic, Sanskrit-like language.

Hmong people believe the body has twelve souls,
each working part—arm, leg, head—possesses a soul,
and when that soul leaves its place in the body,
it would be long lost. If not quickly found,
the part belonging to the lost soul would be weak.

In trance he can travel without distance,
going from one home, one road, to the next,
riding on his horse, the wooden horse. In its physical
appearance, the horse is an ordinary bench,
but to him it is an immovable horse.

Because most soul-spirits are not bound
by time and distance, he can only reach lost souls
while sitting on the wooden horse.

The only time he and the horse will separate
is when a child or animal crosses his
path, the distance between him and his altar—
or when someone tilts over the wooden bench,
causing the rider to fall from his horse.
When this happens—the trance prematurely broken—
he will lose his life if his godfather is not there to help him
regain his captured soul-spirits.

There he is again, speaking fiercely but compassionately
to the heart's soul of a woman, who has been through so many
deaths—the deaths of her son, or her daughter, or her husband.
One can imagine why the heart's soul wanders from the heart.
And, one might imagine the heart's soul replying to the Shaman
when asked why it has left its place on this earth.

# Forest Fire near Mt. Shasta, June 2017

Around the round
    foot of this volcano, if time is

the embers burning
    red like poetry

and if fire is the catalyst for rebirth
for conifers,

    and their budding
green wings flame
up like scarlet butterflies,
      marooning upward in
      the afternoon,
we can live, again—

## How Two Springs Can Grow Fins

We met and I was
a young spring and you
were even younger—

gurgling down
the mountains, passing
by sun and moon—
joined as one river.

Bamboo leaves
sift the wind,

we became the fish
and lived in them,
our becoming turned

gold—oak nearing winter,
and we circle
in the soft eddies—

as the river flows on,
making karst blossoms
from the sky's scaly blue,

flows into the ocean
and on fine days
grow fins.

# The Poem Gary Snyder Wrote

*for Carole*

For a moment the poem he wrote
flutters in the wind crisp sunshine

plummet to when he first came and
learned to live among the hills

the remains of earth and sky
blossoming with pine needles, that

dry twigs left-behind sorrow,
that light green air that comes

and goes in the hot day and cool evening.
He picks up bow and arrow and shoots
the distant bale of hay, arrow flying as if

he found her sitting on their front porch
overlooking the small garden

itself surrounded by mashed fence
to keep in the vegetable, to keep out

deer, bears and squirrels—dark hair
caught on the wire flutters.

## Butterfly Hair in the Sun

Your dimpled, slow-to-bloom smile is what I remember.
Anne, the wind is blowing your butterfly hair in the sun.

I remembered you the afternoon I exited off
Highway 99 into Eight Mile Road:
while realizing that the people at that gas station
stared at me with red-eyes,
I wished you were there with me
so you could shoot their prejudiced looks
with your California poppy smiles.

That feeling wasn't as painful as it was sad when I hear
of the boy you've made an amateur movie with.
You said you and he will be married this December,
but your mother said it will be bad luck to marry in such a season.

I had to agree with her, not because I believed in bad luck,
but because I couldn't tell you not to marry someone else,
because to tell you that would give you a hint about me, unlike
the way you might picture me speaking during regular meetings.

Each day I look at the poppy field
not more than the way I would practice
moving onward without knowing
what has really happened to you.
I recall even in dreams reading "The Crystal Lithium" for you,
thinking like *L'Étranger*, I in my indifference move towards you.

Because I have practiced long and hard not to remember you,
Anne, the wind is blowing your butterfly hair in the sun.

# The Doe, the Brown Trout, and the Gray Squirrel

Once, I shot *ib tug maum mos lwj*,
*Odocoileus hemionus*, hiding behind a tree
blood flowing through the pine needles—

Once, I caught *ib tug ntses*,
*Salmo trutta*, longer than my arm
but did not eat it because the fire
took too long, its flesh
became soft and mushy.

Once, before dawn, I shot *ib tug nas txho*,
*Sciurus griseus*, and wrapped it in a brown bag
like my lunch, placed it deep down
in my backpack and forgot it. Carried it home
in the valley heat, it spoiled and stank, my wife
*xav hais tias* something else had died—

Its death filled the neighborhood;
fearing complaints, *ntshai lawv cem*, I dug
a hole in the garden and let the earth
reclaim its effluvium.

For once, I say a prayer of forgiveness,
listen to the songs of *kuv lub siab*
that I failed to hear before,
and eat what I have killed.

## Little Arrival

*for Lewg*

It's only six months now,
and we're already anxious for you to arrive.

When you arise again to fill the uneven space
left by those before me, who have passed in order
for you to return to this world or by those
who had journeyed far and long and
disappeared into the soil which sustains us all,

when you arise from out of your amniotic shell,
unlike the rising of the second coming of the One
whom some believe had forgotten or forsaken
them, but like the rising of a sunflower in the field,
colorful as this season and many seasons to live,

when you ascend to the surface from your
nurturing place, placed there by me, who
in turn was placed here by wanderers whom I must learn not to love
and to love something from them to you by way of the seeds in me,

when you emerge into the light of either night or day,
just as those of us in this room once had,
not realizing that you have arrived when you are arriving,

when you arise after long months of becoming you,
of becoming becoming or of becoming one ready to enter this
world, that you might one day be holding close
to the door of a girl whom you'll love,
there only to wait for re-entrance to the house of this Earth,
when, in this body, I may no longer be able to see,

when you arise like crossing the rushing river, red
water rushes along with you, and you
making your first cry, a sadness or an awakening,
which may be the only sign of
calling to the spirits, I have arrived,

when you keep on arising throughout this life,
and my moments have been risen forward, because I have already
served to link with you the gifts of many, for you
whom I have loved or will love more than this body,
love in more ways than the way through which we keep on arising.

## The Whitetails

Light had yet to make lines
in the sky, when a young Hmong hunter trailed
into a patch of young pines.

Then, he saw a pair of gesturing antlers pointing
into heaven, long ears flapping
away gnats, three of them—fawn, doe, and buck;
for a moment, it was like a long
stare between two peoples of
a dividing country—

and the young hunter held up
his rifle to capture through the scope the sight
that is already a fading red painting
in the wind on a snowy field;
he sat back, down on the wet
ground that had been dust.

# A Love Poem

*by Soul Vang*

The waves form a constant roar,
As if they would crash through

The western picture windows.
A man receives a phone call

From his four-year-old son
Unable to sleep without saying "Good night!"

The man steps out to the patio
And holds the phone towards the sea.

"Do you hear the noise?" he asks.
"Daddy is at the ocean."

All that is left

All that is left
Of the dead seal

Is a pile of gray
Defoliating skin.

As waves recede
Two rocks rise

Out of a desert-
Like landscape.

A chip of dragon tooth,
Pounded by a million waves,

Slowly grinds
Into sand.

# Mother of Myths

*by Khaty Xiong*

The tree can't stand to look—
the overbearing mistress of a cloud
heading straight for the mountain—
the mountains misty again
    after her five hundred deaths.
Lo, the poor, bastard of a child weaving
right through the arrow of her spine,
swinging from one rib to the end
    of her threaded thigh bone,
screaming in terrible splendor
shrill bets against his life on earth,
vows taken in by the sun, transformed
    into pomelos and papayas.
Down here, the flowers care not
to comment, the peevish streams caught
in a basin of their own wicked making.
    In place of the land's language,
a vague dream—horses slashing
through wild rice, past opium meadows,
past mangled bodies of lustrous hemp—
    the beasts trotting in the sea
of their monstrous sorrows sown from birth
and in the felled arms of the mighty sky.
There in the ruins of their hurry, an ape
    chanting, there are no masters left!
The ape, a masterless loom of a hundred
years settled on the rock of a *vaub kib*,
traveling at the speed of a withering spirit.
    Why does the tree not look?
Can it not see the mother is dead?
Can it not know the child is alone?

Higher in the clouds more witnesses—
    snakes wrestling in symmetry,
their tongues breaking truce in tandem,
spoiling wet their unborn livers, pathless
civilians drawing names they will wear.

# IV

## Mountain Spirits

## Inclusions: What Is Not Me

I sit alone on a bench,
To watch the world outside of me.

A black crow,
Some say it is a sign of something,
Flies overhead, then
Lands on a pine branch.

This sad, wooden bench,
Nobody realizing its lively
Presence, is not me.
These things are not me.

The trees standing high
With leaves,

Or the quiet, unknown wind
That trims my hair
Like the Chinese lady barber
That fades away, a calm silence,
Or a whisper, is not me.

The man who yells fiercely to his
Beautiful shepherd dog, to carry the Frisbee
In its mouth across the Memorial Union sidewalk, is not me.
This man's heart is not mine.

Matthew the handsome poet
Who greets me with "Writing Poem?"
But not stopping to chat,

And the European man
With dark sun glasses,
Carrying a red bag,
Walking, eyes on his feet,
Indifferent to my presence,
Is not this person sitting alone forever?

The bike-impounding officer
With shorts and a white helmet,
Walking towards the Coffee House,
Dragging a neon-green bicycle
To an appropriate parking area,
Although he is the law
He is not me.

A beautiful Chinese lady
Approaches me
And smiles, as if she
Wants to share a secret.
But as she nears,
She walks onward.

I want to call after her
And make good love to her.

But they are sadly not me forever.

# The Spirit and the Undead

In the barley plains of
North Dakota shall we
pray lowly like stones
   in the sun-bathed
      hills?   Or shall we lay
         down like      a single poem
         abandoned      on a chair
         in the great      empty hall
         of Minnesota?
      And after everyone      has left, are we lovers
   wrapped in a thin cloud      of silk, fogs that we are
have we forgotten there's      a door left open
for death?

## Days with Sunlight

Do not follow me
to that stony, ancestral land,

but take flight towards the sea,
the rippling, dancing sea, to mountains
capped with daylight that make you want to cry
for their richness.

Head to the shores of Ithaca where poets
are paraded with great homecomings sung
by friends, tables laden with oven-roasted fish,
or wrapped and baked in banana leaves

moistened with seaweed, overflowing
with wild mushrooms, pungent mints
and many nights of love.

# The Dog and the Lady

What am I to the hungry thighs of a lady?
Am I a wandering dog?

She too is human, hungers for someone,
to kiss her back, or smooth her floating hair.
She too hungers for winter's end
as the dove hungers for the first leaf.

A blessing, no one will convince her
with flaming hands that life is well.

I wander, and am always hungry.
And who is this dog?

The night my father, with dew in his eyes,
threw me out into a December street, said,
"You're nothing but a dog—a sad dog howling
your prayers filling the night sky."

These words sliced open my heart.
I sobbed in the street.

In a world of our skins and hungers
this pimple-faced dog and this lady have what is left over,

some part of love that has survived.

# A Memory in November

A day is like the wind flowing by,
a maple leaf like a house
on turbulent water,
like a house full of colors
      hard as desert soil.

      He loves her in the sunlight
and, under moonlight,
watches the leaf

in the mountain streams, passing on
to rivers and lakes and
eventually oceans
      and, if God wills,

      we shall know
in the wind, in the leaf,
in the rains.

## Poem to Sin Myriad

How swelling delicious
    you are in the evening

Light. Naked, plain may be
    the soft hills of Mariposa,

But your breasts, your soft
    curvatures, that torso where

Rivers meet, my sin silk near,
    rough cotton:

Your manzanita scent,
    my revolting, doomed marrows.

## Manzanita Before Winter

Before I breathe my
last breath, you need
to know

I want flame to scour
these fingers,

cremate these pimples
& scars clean to the bone,

all that is skeletal, to be
set on a smooth table,

of cool morning,
a waking atop
the high Sierras,

the smell of pines
& angelic manzanitas budding

&, please, do
let it be ashes,

like a poem revised
to entice you.

## Daim Nplooj / The Leaf

*Tiv nag, koj taub hau hnyo lug lawm,*
*taug txoj niag kev kho siab khuav*
*rov los rau hauv Xeevkhuam*

*Xav zoj xwb, kuv xav caum koj qab.*
*Lub hav zoov dav thiab nqha, ua rau*
*kuv xav pom dua koj lub plhu*

*Tabsis hav zoov nplooj zeeg tas,*
*kuv lub siab dai vias txoj hlua*
*kablaug sab ntawm ib nta ntuj*

*vim ceeb tsheej siab tshaj roob,*
*lub ntiaj teb no muaj koj ib leeg xwb*
*ib nthwv cua thiaj li los ntsawj koj lawm.*

*Zoo li lub pob ntoo qhuav qhawv ntawm*
*no, tus kuv hlub, txhua lub sijhawm,*
*koj yog kuv daim nplooj os mog.*

Your head bowed straight toward
that long sad walk back
to Xiengkhouang in rain

and I yearned to follow you.
The forest is emptied and I
yearn for you, even more.

As the leaf falls on the ground,
my heart, held by
a thinly web, dangles in mid-air,

for Heaven is mountains high,
earth is only you,
the wind sent to snatch you away.

Like this old, parched tree,
sweet in all my
remaining days, you're my leaf.

## Release

I'll seek no veneration or pompous
memorial—only freedom. I'll leave

no attachment or cling to the dharma;
only dissolve into an ideal cumulus,

night's warm blanket over me again,
a recital of earth, sky, and home.

## Poem to the Setting Sun

If I am to die
    let me go gently
    like the setting

evening sun,

the night and darkness
    will be my eyes closing.

## Hours of Hunger

I am eaten, consumed
by a winter that covers,

its devouring consumes
even the sweet grass where
I once held you in a nest of hay.

I remain beautiful with you.

Feed me your delicate, lovely hours
before I'm consumed.

## Karst Mountains Will Bloom

The sun will set, the moon wane,
earth will be as the forest during autumn,
stars at night will blossom like summer lilies.

The leaves will never yellow
and fall, fading, like grandmother's tears.

The robins will resonate
to wind-court my grandfather's lonely day.

But, if you could love me,
Karst Mountains will bloom—

# Poem No One Likes

*for my son Forest*

I want to write
a poem
that you may not like—

it is a poem
you might want to
tear into pieces

because it is a poem
about death
& goodbyes,

because it is a poem
of sorrow & wailing
prognosis for my tomorrow,

but please let me
finish it with
the color of a leaf

in the spring &
when it ripens
in autumn

like a plump
sweet peach in my garden,
you may choose

to dismember or consume it
like setting love &
the Buddha into fire—

when this poem is, or
when I am, white & gray
ashes in the crematory,

this poem, bold inks of my
morning, will raise
up my soul like clouds

impermanent in your
beautiful palm, & your
tender, scholarly fingers

will write of me with taints
of primroses & tears,
about my sad bamboo

shoots for a million
elephants in the Great
Plains of Luang Prabang,

with an artistry, the pen
of your hand.
I shall not cave into

oblivion nor be left
among the waves of
wind, or the waves over

the radio of my favorite
songs—my love, even if all
these were not true, you

have now finished the poem
you so did not like
to begin with

and I wake from my long
silent sleep to the tone of your
usual, "O Dad, did you know?"

## Monument

*by Mai Der Vang*

What is the name for an antelope
   who grazes inside a dream

then vanishes into the
            nebula's brush.

        What is the face
for refurbishing grammar

       at each comma's lip.
       Whose identity never

remembers the shape of beige.
  What is the word

          for how to conjure
    the sigh of a line hushed

   beneath the flap of a thousand
shifting plumes.

What is the body of a
      garden where a crescent

        despairs, drifts beneath
the melt of amber.

The season is always growing
out its hooves.

One cradlesong
of your leaving is not larger

than the forest of your arrival.
*To make you a noun forever.*

A loss of you
cannot be equal to the loss of you.

# The Jump

*by Jer Xiong*

You say to me,
"Write more than we can dream."

As a child,
I scaled an oak tree, limb by limb,
to the widest branch.
I clung to the twigs,
towering above my sisters,
enjoying the thrill of a first climb.

After a moment,
my sisters jumped off, one by one,
from branches to grass.
I stared at their forms
like frogs landing on lily pads,
natural for experienced climbers.

I did not let go,
unable to give up the things
that held me steady.
I stayed on the bough,
waiting for the right timing,
but it would not come until I move.

Your words remind me of stepping off that edge:
In mid-air, a sense of certainty that I will make it.

# A Poet's Note

The Laotian landscape of my childhood was a nomadic landscape. I recollect soft hills, abundant with long grass and foot trails. Views from our mountain looked out to villages along the river. Woods and brush, cut and burning, transforming ash into fertile fields. Green rice fields, creeks dripping, rain and sunshine on water buffaloes grazing, my village like so many others.

It was sad to have been forced out of our mountains and fields by the danger of the raging Secret War. My own *Yaw*, my grandfather, didn't like fighting. He was a casualty and died, abandoned somewhere along the road to America. Fleeing this presence of war we began to dream, to imagine a landscape where poppy flowers grew under a warm sun and we might sleep in a barn of sweet hay, to gaze up, unafraid at a night sky with a clear blue moon.

Writing poems in American has always been as difficult as climbing a mountain or swimming across a strong river. I think that my writing differs from the "native" American speaker's in that a native speaker will quickly catch the awkwardness of my writing. I owe my rhythms to all the past poets whose works I have read or whose musical, heart-felt lines I have sung out. It also has something to do with what one gets from descending, and ascending a "mountain," crossing a river without a bridge. Whether ascending or descending, the struggle intrigues me; it feels both joyful and meaningful.

Like mountains, rivers also represent a boundary in both the spiritual and physical sense. One must cross a river in order to reach "one's home." The crossing of this "water without end" became part of our Hmong diaspora. Along this journey, traveling out of the mountains and plains of Laos to cross the Mekong River, there were so many deaths and much suffering. But death and suffering are welcome;

they are merely one challenge to our people's spiritual and physical endurance.

My poetry comes out of the suffering of being forced to leave those mountains which had for centuries been shelters for my ancestors. Soldiers who wanted our silver and gold, our hard labor, our mountains and fields and rivers, drove us away with their bombs and bullets.

I believe my poems depict a universal and all too common struggle. I do not look at the mountains we ascended and descended, the rivers we crossed, or the burdens (sometimes family, friends, or strangers) we carried as heavy loads that caused me suffering, or as suffering inflicted upon me and my people. I only want to remember that the mountains sheltered us, and always will, like the Buddha who tries to keep sentient beings "awake."

Our new life in the central part of California has blessed me with some of the joys which I feared might be lost. Living close to the Sierra Nevada, I feel the mountains' beauty and power. Working as a seasonal firefighter along the Merced River headwaters, I came to feel a deep affection for this region, happy that so many of my fellow Hmong had chosen to make their new lives here.

I want my words to hold a torch up to illuminate the culture of my people: my wife's and her mother's weaving, the good taste of a fresh-caught fish prepared our way, our gardens dark with the green spicy leaves in which we wrap our food. I want to teach my sons and daughters our old ways, the traditional rituals on walks in these new mountains, beside these blue rivers, through these oak and pine forests, and to worship the animals and rocks. I pray our old ways will not be lost, or fade, that our children and their children will know something from our old lives, to live peacefully with each other and with the spirits.

I grew up with half of my life spent in a country in which I couldn't decipher the sound of a letter even if it were printed as bold as large as an elephant, so I developed a taste for the juiciness of words late in my life. Now I long to write of the poetic shades of my life and home—foothills, mountains, cities, people, and wildlife—because while I live, I see not only the seasonal rhythms of spring greens and autumn rising and falling in layers of gold, orange, the creamy yellow on the mountain trails, but also all of life's intricacies, its give and take, its death and renewal.

I believe poetic transcendence does not require extraordinary feats from any poet. The poet needs only to be ordinary, to have forded rivers of hardship remaining patient and truthful to the pains and joys of one's life. All through my writing days, I have admired the literary masters of the past. I have been inspired to be near them, like pausing near the foot of a grand mountain before slowly climbing. I only know that poetry has been my sure way, helping me ascend and understand a little of my life.

Writing workshops at UC Davis and with my friends at the Hmong American Writers' Circle (HAWC) nurtured my passion for words and their cadences. I learned that poetry occurs at the fine line between sun and moon, between evenings alone and days under the scorching sun. It appears in rare moments when I began to "see" with my heart. I have had great teachers. Gary Snyder, my thoughtful mentor who has traversed across many countries and has been my guide to wild living and the "old ways." My friend and "literary mother" Sandra McPherson's honest and profound poetry continues to show me the right path.

If I am ever risen, a kindred spirit to these predecessors, I imagine it will be like a long, contemplative repose, a clear river below, on the heights and crevices of an open, icy mountain. Oh, those karst China mountains, those jagged peaks, like a poet's pen aimed towards the heaven in my heart.

## Notes

"Hours of Hunger" and "Eating" are poems the poet wrote during his experience with radiation treatment.

"Karst Mountains Will Bloom" in its original form was written in the Hmong Romanized Popular Alphabet, and the poem's last line was first translated by poet Soul Vang to English as the title to the gala reading in Merced, California, in 2016. The poem in Hmong was later translated by the poet here.

"The Old Man by the Road They Go": *Pi-nyu-waih*—a fist-size baboon-like animal that inhabits the forest. The Hmong people fear its extraordinary, magical power. When a hunter comes in close contact with one of these creatures (i.e., hears one of them howl or shake the forest), its "curse" causes the hunter death in one or two days if the proper rituals are not observed.

"The Ritual before Crossing the River": This ritual is significant to the Hmong because it is here that, when we tried to cross to Thailand during our exodus, hundreds and perhaps thousands of Hmong perished. We arrived at the river very thirsty and hungry. From my experience as a little boy, I don't recall that we actually drank from the river, but from pools along the river. When we drank we recalled the sources of reincarnation or rebirth as coming from this river. Thus, in drinking from it, should you die, you are presumed to enter into, or perhaps through, one of the two sources: only through suffering will one reach nirvana, or only through blissful desire will one find sorrow. Here are choices, and in making these choices we create our next incarnation.

"The One Sitting on His Wooden Horse": Physically, in the present world, he appears immovable, or people are afraid to move him; spirit-wise, he travels unbounded.

# Thanks To

At Blue Oak Press, **Randy White**. I'd like to say in the highest Hmong aphorism: *"Kuv nco koj txiaj ntsim mus txhis"* (My gratitude to you is forever ingrained into memory) like the karst mountain, Mt. Kailash, rising. I could not have found an editor and friend who has dedicated more love into publishing than the way I have seen you place on this book. Thanks also to **Josh McKinney**, editor at Blue Oak Press, for your keen attunement and careful consideration of each poem. To **Maxima Kahn**, whose artistic touch and design brought the cover to life.

At UC Davis, **Sandra McPherson**, big-loving-heart literary mother; you were first to believe in my literary voice, and your guidance has led these poems to fruition. You have worked on my behalf in ways I may never know. To **Gary Snyder**, my grand teacher-poet and friend, who continues to guide me into the Sierra Nevada mountains in many of these poems. Your guidance and suggestions for improving this collection make it eternally special. You taught me that I, too, can live on Turtle Island and set my heart to earth and sky beyond the cosmos. To **Alan B. Williamson**, my professor who patiently *took* me by the hands and taught me to understand poetry and remained my first true essayist and "muse of distance."

To **Boon Ma Yang**. You're our community's rare Hmong artist and painter. To **Lee Herrick**, my longtime friend and Poet Laureate of Fresno. Your praise glitters this book with kindness and beauty. To **Mai Der Vang** and **Anthony Cody**, my most thoughtful critics in our group of writers; you are both dear friends, and I learned to listen well from you. Thank you for continuing to enjoy my poetry and to inspire me to march on with my pen. To **Andre Yang**, HAWC founder, my writing confidante; you're my spokesperson, always. To **Burlee** and **Mary Vang**, who sought me out and connected me to the writing communities; you both are early joint supporters of all my writing. **Burlee**, your words add joy to this collection. To **Yu-Han Chao**, a friend of poets everywhere, more so to me; you worked tirelessly to help revise and organize the original manuscript and set it on the right path. To **Jer Xiong**, whose praise and enthusiasm in writing energize me. To **Yia Lee** you are the best addition to HAWC, and I have enjoyed reading with you. Your fun literary voice will shine. To **Khaty Xiong**, whose sadness and pains are shared in all my days; let your poetry pave the path toward love and healing. To **Max Hallman**, philosopher, friend, and teacher who has guided me through my early college days; your scholarly direction points the way. To **Se** and **Cho Kue**—we are few but we may do better to measure the world with love and have the courage to rise forth. To **Vinnie Lee**, my brother who drives me from Merced to San Francisco for medical treatment in rain and in sunshine; I am sincere because of you. To **Nini Lee**, the sister I know I have; thank you for your support in my dire times.

Friends and members of Merced's local support organizations, Southeast Vision for Education (SAVE) and Southeast Asian-American Professionals Association (SEA-APA); thank you all for your support and recognition of my literary work and your philanthropic contributions to the educational needs of our community's youth.

## Acknowledgments

Some of these poems have appeared in the following publications, and grateful acknowledgement is made to their editors.

*Swan Scythe Press*: "Open Hands and the Man with One Leg Shorter," "Passing at the Canyon," "The Old Man by the Road They Go," "The People beneath a Moon by the River," "The Ritual before Crossing the River," "Spokane, Washington, 1980," "Something about Yaw," "Laos, 1977," "The World Has Always Been beyond Me," "The One Sitting on His Wooden Horse," "Inclusions: What Is Not Me," "The Dog and the Lady," "These Would Have Been Days to Be," "Butterfly Hair in the Sun," "By the Lake in Which I Love You," "Little Arrival," and "Returning to Mountain: A Brief Aesthetic"

*Yang Design, HmongStory 40 Exhibit, 2016*: "The Ritual before Crossing the River"

*Lantern Review: A Journal of Asian American Poetry*: "The Whitetails"

*Heyday Books*: "A Memory in November," "Between You and the Sea," and "These Would Have Been Days"

*River Press*: "Open Hands and the Man with One Leg Shorter," "Passing at the Canyon," "The Old Man by the Road They Go," "The People beneath a Moon by the River," and "The Ritual before Crossing the River"

*Poetry*: "Monument" by Mai Der Vang

A special acknowledgement to *Hmong Textile Designs* by Anthony Chan, published by Stemmer House Publishers of Gilsum, New Hampshire, for the Hmong textile designs used on the section pages.

## About Cover Artist Boon Ma Yang

Known throughout Hmong communities in the United States as a painter and freelance illustrator, Boon Ma Yang is among the first generation of refugees from Laos. He was born in 1983 in Xieng Khouang, Laos. He and his family immigrated to the United States in 1991. Currently, he and his wife and children reside in Atwater, California.

Boon Ma received his Bachelor of Arts in Painting and Drawing from the Academy of Arts, University of San Francisco. His painting technique not only focuses on the application of paints but also is influenced by contemporary street artists and by the illustrator and painter, Norman Rockwell. His painting for the cover of *Karst Mountains Will Bloom* is titled *"Zos Roob Tsua Zeb,"* in English "Karst Mountain Village."

His work has been donated to Hmong community events (such as Refugee Day) fundraising for non-profit organizations. For the past eight years, his paintings, graphics, and murals have captured thematic elements related to Hmong spiritual cosmology, belief, and ritual practices in Shamanism as well as depicting the Hmong's landscape and agrarian life in Laos and Thailand. Some of Boon Ma's works have been published in Yang Design's widely distributed *TXHAWB* magazine.

Boon Ma Yang's most recent exhibit was part of the elaborate Hmong Story 40 Exhibit in Fresno, Merced, and Sacramento, in which he provided visuals of the Hmong's traumatic Diaspora experience during the Secret War in Laos. His work has influenced political ideologies and brought about human rights awareness inspiring the next generation of young Hmong artists.

## About Pos Moua

Pos Moua lives in Merced, California, with his wife and five children. He is a language arts teacher who has taught Hmong and English at Merced High School and Merced College for about twenty years. His first chapbook, *Where The Torches Are Burning* (Swan Scythe Press, 2001) gives "an account of love and family and identity in the poet's new land." His poems have appeared in the anthologies *Tilting the Continent: Southeast Asian American Writing* (New Rivers Press, 2000) and *How Do I Begin?: A Hmong American Literary Anthology* (Heyday Books, 2011).

# About the Contributing Writers

**Gary Snyder** has published numerous books of poetry and prose, including *Axe Handles*, for which he received an American Book Award, and *Turtle Island*, which won the Pulitzer Prize. He has received many awards including an American Academy of Arts and Letters Award, the Bollingen Prize, a Guggenheim Foundation fellowship, the Ruth Lilly Poetry Prize, and the Shelley Memorial Award. Snyder was elected a Chancellor of the Academy of American Poets in 2003 and was the recipient of the 2012 Wallace Stevens Award for lifetime achievement by the Academy of American Poets. He is a retired professor of English from the University of California, Davis.

**Sandra McPherson's** books include twelve with Ecco, Wesleyan, Illinois, and Ostrakon. Her newest collection, *Quicksilver, Cougars, and Quartz*, will be published in 2019 by Salmon Poetry Press (Ireland). New work will be found in *The Iowa Review, Field, Poetry, Ecotone, Plume, Basalt, Agni, Antioch Review, Ploughshares, Red Wheelbarrow*, and *Epoch*. She taught twenty-three years at University of California, Davis and four at the Iowa Writers' Workshop. She founded and edited Swan Scythe Press. Her honors include two grants from the Ingram Merrill Foundation, three National Endowment of the Arts fellowships, a Guggenheim Foundation fellowship, and an award in literature from the American Academy and Institute of Arts and Letters. Her poetry was also featured in the PBS special, *The Language of Life*, hosted by Bill Moyers. It was her pleasure to work at UCD with Pos Moua from the time he came into her office and introduced himself through his graduation from the Masters program in Creative Writing.

**Mai Der Vang** is the author of *Afterland* (Graywolf Press, 2017), winner of the 2016 Walt Whitman Award from the Academy of American Poets. The recipient of a Lannan Literary Fellowship, her poetry has appeared or is forthcoming in *Poetry*, *Tin House*, the *American Poetry Review*, among other journals and anthologies. In Fall 2019, Mai Der will join the Creative Writing MFA faculty at Fresno State as an Assistant Professor of English in Creative Writing.

**Yu-Han Chao** was born and grew up in Taipei, Taiwan, and received her MFA from Penn State University. Her short story collection, *Sex and Taipei City*, is available from Red Hen Press. The Backwaters Press, Dancing Girl Press, BOAAT, Imaginary Friend Press, and Another New Calligraphy have published her other poetry collections and chapbooks. More information can be found at www.yuhanchao.com and her blog at yuhanchao.blogspot.com.

**Burlee Vang** is the author of *The Dead I Know: Incantation for Rebirth* (Swan Scythe Press, 2010) and coeditor of *How Do I Begin?: A Hmong American Literary Anthology* (Heyday, 2011). His prose and poetry have also appeared in *Ploughshares*, *Alaska Quarterly Review*, and *North American Review*, among other journals. Also a filmmaker, he was awarded the Academy of Motion Picture Arts and Sciences' 2011 Nicholl Award. He teaches at Long Beach City College and lives in Cerritos, California.

**Khaty Xiong** is a Hmong American poet who hails from Fresno, California. She is the author of *Poor Anima* (Apogee Press, 2015) and three poetry chapbooks: *Ode to the Far Shore* (Platypus Press, 2016), *Deer Hour* (New Michigan Press, 2014), and *Elegies* (University of Montana, 2013). She has received a fellowship from MacDowell Colony and a grant from the Ohio Arts Council. Her work has been published in *Poetry*, the *New York Times*, *How Do I Begin?: A Hmong American Literary Anthology*, and elsewhere.

**Jer Xiong** is a Hmong American from Chico, California. She received her BA in English at CSU, Chico, and is currently an MFA student at

CSU, Fresno, focusing on creative nonfiction. She has been a writing tutor, a youth mentor, and a first-year writing instructor. She has also been a student editor for *Watershed Review* and an intern for *The Normal School*. She is a member of the Hmong American Writers' Circle.

# Blue Oak Press Literature Series

The Blue Oak Literature Series embraces the breadth of culture, ethnicity, and geography of the American West by publishing and promoting works by both new and established writers and poets.

## A Note on the Type

The text of this book was set in elegant Centaur, the only typeface designed by Bruce Rodgers (1870–1957), the well-known American book designer. Rodgers based his design on the Roman face cut by Nicolas Jenson in 1470 for his Oxford Bible. The italic used to accompany Centaur is Arrighi based on the chancery face used by Lodovico degli Arrighi in 1524.